WHAT ARE THE COUNTRIES IN THE EUROPEAN UNION?

Geography Books for Kids
Children's Geography & Culture Books

Speedy Publishing LLC

40 E. Main St. #1156

Newark, DE 19711

www.speedypublishing.com

Copyright 2017

What is the European Union?
What countries are members?
Let's find out!

FLAGS OF THE EUROPEAN UNION

THE EUROPEAN UNION

The European Union, or EU, is an economic and political union of twenty-eight nations, most of them in Europe. Over 500 million people live in EU member states, and its territory is more than 1.7 million square miles. The EU supports free movement of people, goods, services, and money among its members.

The EU has helped member countries avoid conflicts, including disputes that might lead to war. It is a remarkable achievement that countries like France and Germany, which were military rivals for centuries, now cooperate in the EU as partners and allies.

JOINT NEWS CONFERENCE FOLLOWING RUSSIAN-FRENCH-GERMAN TALKS

The EU has a series of decision-making bodies that help develop policies and resolve conflicts. They include the European

Parliament, the Court of Justice, and the European Central Bank.

A nation that belongs to the EU must bring its laws and policy into harmony with EU laws. EU members must agree unanimously on matters involving military action or political or trade agreements with non-EU members.

The EU is one of the largest economic units in the world, and is sometimes described as the "newest superpower".

WHO NEEDS THE EU?

The history of Europe is full of wars and economic struggles between nations. Both the large countries, like France and England, and small countries like the Netherlands, have fought hard to protect themselves and to expand their rights and power both in Europe and around the world.

THE BATTLE BETWEEN AUSTRO-BAVARIAN
AND FRENCH FORCES

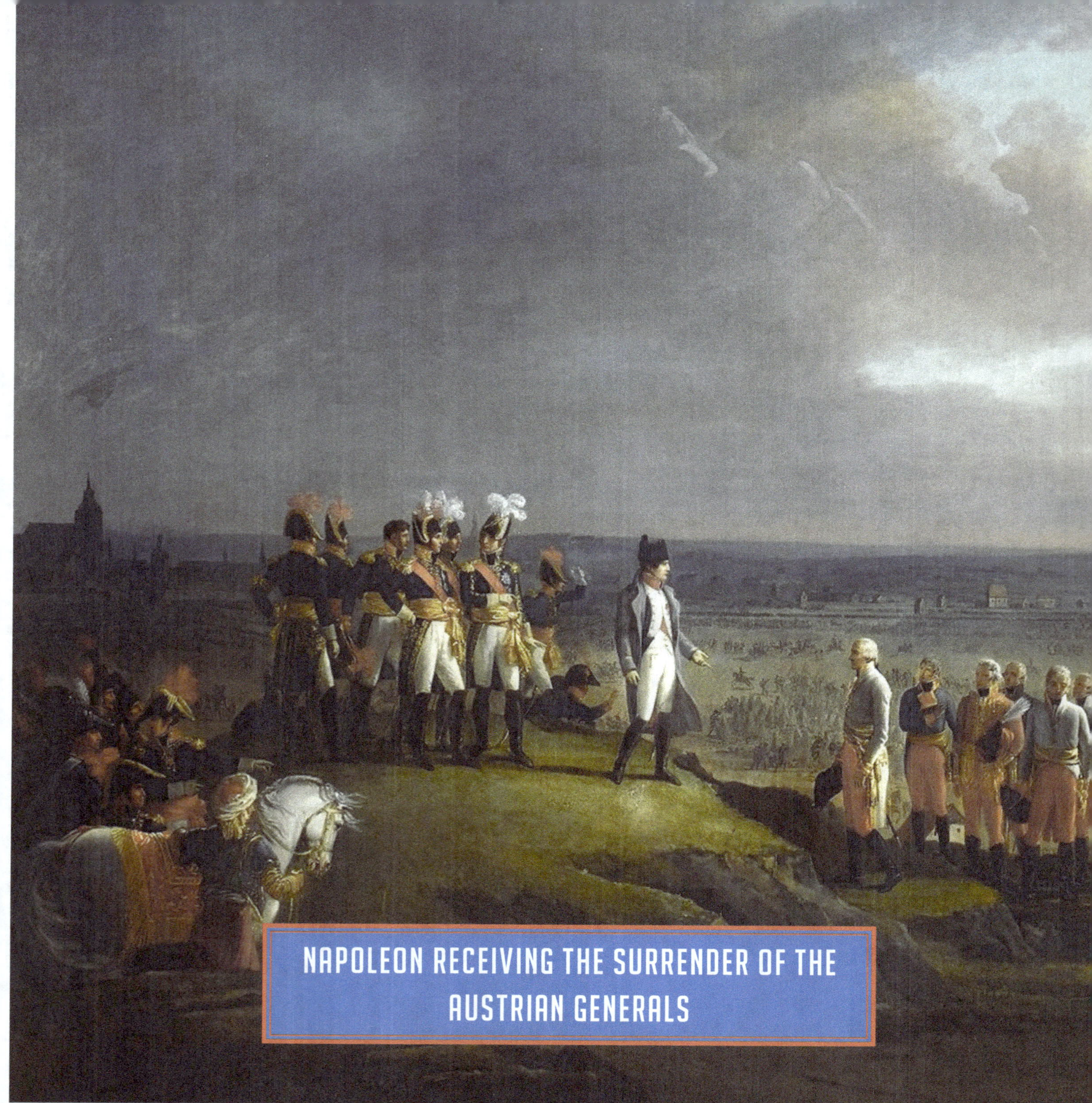
NAPOLEON RECEIVING THE SURRENDER OF THE AUSTRIAN GENERALS

This competition between states has not been friendly. It has led to huge wars over and over again. Read the Baby Professor book Royals Hold Grudges for 100 Years! to learn about a war that went on for over a century between Europe's great powers.

Some of these wars were driven by resentment and fear. The small German states only unified into one large state, Germany, late in the 19th century. Italy had a similar history. These two countries felt that England, Spain, and France, which had unified much earlier and had developed colonies in much of the world, had an unfair advantage. Germany, in particular felt that it was hemmed in by France in the west and Russia in the east. German politicians repeatedly called for "lebensraum", room to live in.

AN 18TH-CENTURY VIEW OF VENICE

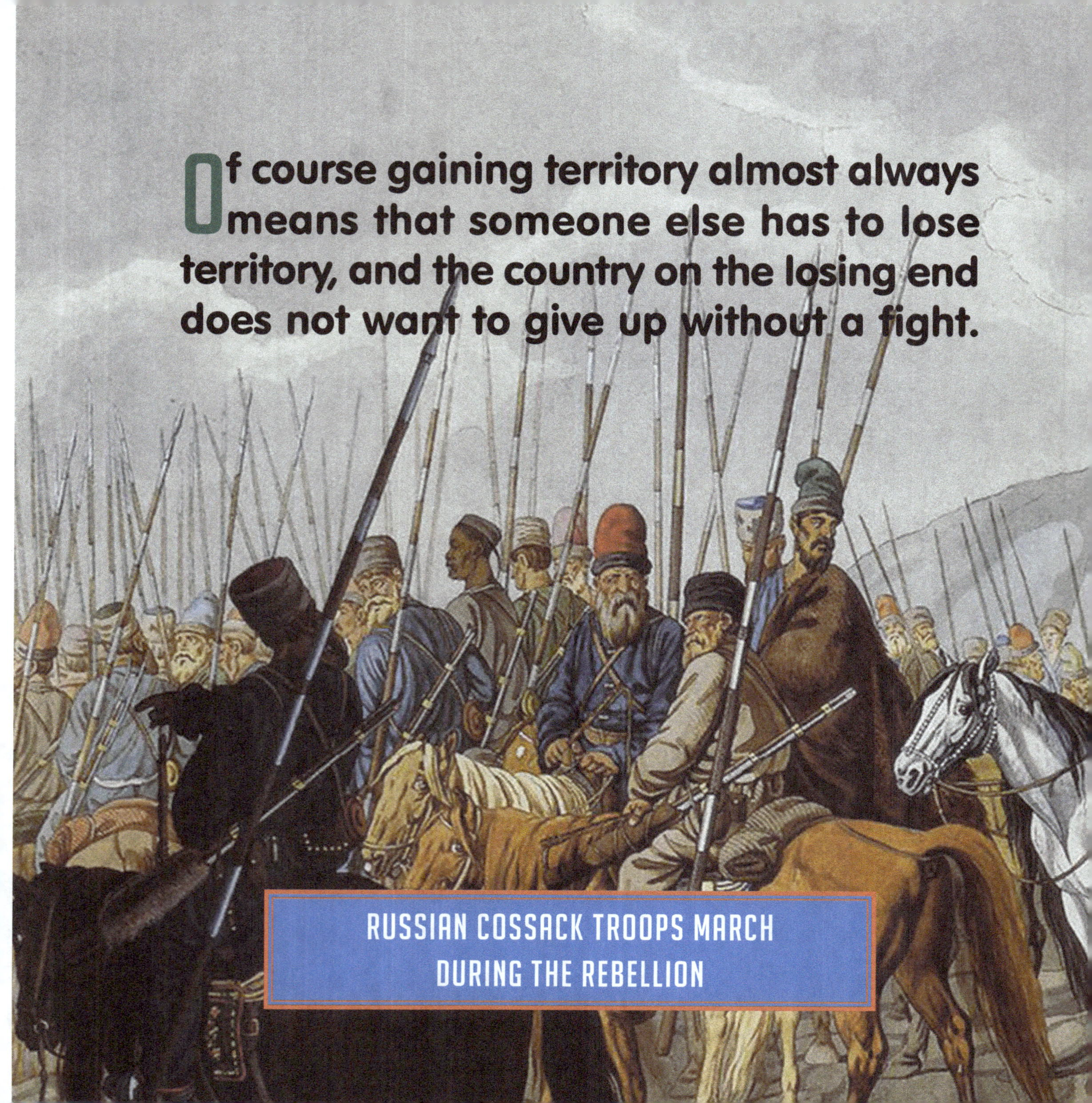

Of course gaining territory almost always means that someone else has to lose territory, and the country on the losing end does not want to give up without a fight.

Europe suffered through war after war over hundreds of years, right up to the twentieth century.

At the end of World War I in 1918, at the urging of US President Woodrow Wilson, nations tried to build a structure that would help countries resolve difficulties peacefully, and learn to work together better. The first attempt was the League of Nations. It was a weak association with no power to enforce its rulings, and some strong countries did not join it, so the League did not do much to slow the march toward World War II.

PRESIDENT WOODROW WILSON

EUROPE READY AND WAITING FOR D-DAY,
WORLD WAR II

During and after World War II, from 1939 to 1945, countries made a second attempt to develop an international body that would give countries a place to work out their disagreements without calling out the army. The United Nations has had a strong record of success in reducing or preventing conflicts since the Korean War, which ended in 1953.

The United Nations operates on a global scale, and deals with issues that affect all countries. The European Union is an attempt to work the same way for the countries of Europe, reducing possible points of conflict and helping former rivals work together for the common good. It, also, has had a very good record of success.

UNITED NATIONS
UNITED FOR PEACE AND FREEDOM

EUROPEAN UNION
CORPORATE TAX MAKEOVER

Apart from reducing the chance of war, the EU helps reduce barriers to travel, trade, and the sharing of ideas. Before the European Union existed, a business in one country had to deal with more than 20 often-conflicting sets of rules governing imports, exports, and taxes. Now these rules are harmonized to reduce costs, simplify business, and improve people's access to goods.

1957

The European Union began with six member nations forming the European Economic Community. These were Belgium, France, Italy, the Netherlands, Luxembourg, and West Germany.

VISITEURS &
FOURNISSEURS
P
VISITEURS
OFFICIELS

EAST BERLIN "DEATH STRIP" OF THE BERLIN WALL, 1984

1973

In the first expansion of the EU, Great Britain, Ireland, and Denmark were admitted.

1981

Greece joined the EU.

1986

Portugal and Spain became EU members.

1990

When West Germany reunited with East Germany, the number of EU member states did not increase, but the EU's population grew by over 16 million people.

1995

The next expansion welcomed Austria, Finland, and Sweden.

2004

Eight of the ten countries that joined this year were formerly part of the Soviet Union, or of the Eastern Bloc of states allied to the Soviet Union. They were The Czech Republic, Estonia, Hungary, Latvia, Lithuania, Poland, Slovakia, and Slovenia.

The other states joining the EU this year were Malta and Cyprus.

VIGILIA PRETIUM LIBERTATIS

SUPREME HEADQUARTERS
ALLIED POWERS EUROPE

CROATIA

2007

This year two more former allies of the Soviet Union, Bulgaria and Romania, joined the EU.

2013

In 2013 Croatia, a nation that had been part of Yugoslavia and part of the Eastern Bloc, joined the EU.

TRANSITIONS

Greenland is a part of Denmark, but is largely self-governing. In 1979, Greenland voted to leave all European institutions, and completed its exit from the EU in 1985.

GREENLAND

Several countries are in the process of bringing their laws, border controls, and economic activity in line with the EU so they can become full members. They are

MONTENEGRO

former Eastern Bloc members Albania,
Montenegro, Serbia, and Macedonia and
Turkey.

The EU established the Copenhagen Criteria for candidate nations: to join the organization, a nation must have a democratic government with free elections, have a "free" economic system rather than tight state control, and honor the Universal Declaration of Human Rights and the rule of law.

NYHAVN COPENHAGEN

SCOTLAND

In 2016 the UK voted for Brexit: the nickname for Great Britain leaving the European Union. They began the formal process of leaving in 2017. Scotland, a part of Great Britain, is working on a plan to remain part of the EU.

THE EUROZONE

Nineteen of the EU's 28 members belong to the "Eurozone", which simplifies trade between countries. The Eurozone supports free movement of goods, services, people, and money between its member countries.

Each of these Eurozone countries used to have its own currency. Now they share a common currency, the Euro. Its symbol is €.

EUROZONE

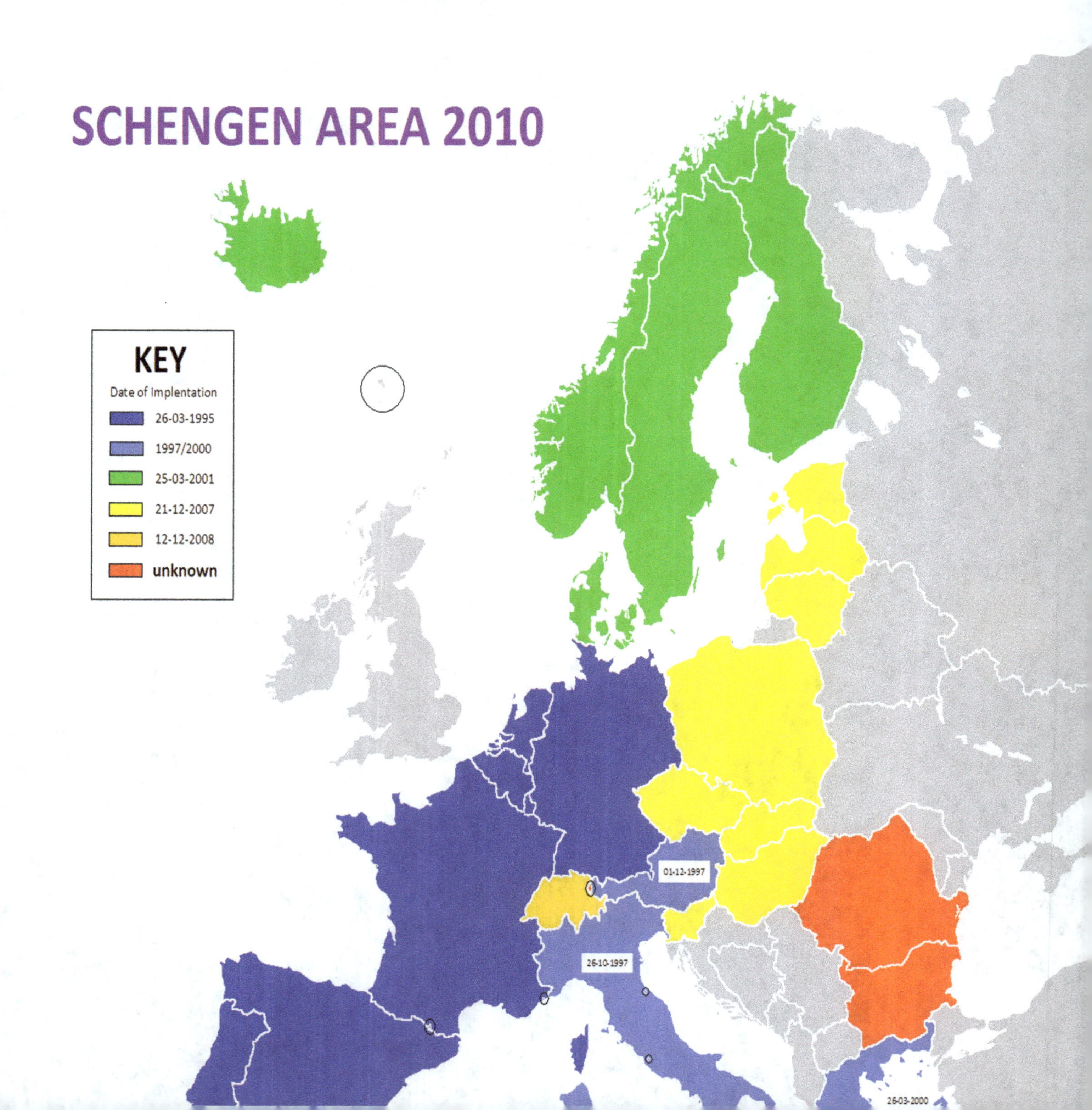

SCHENGEN AREA 2010
KEY
Date of Implentation
26-03-1995
1997/2000
25-03-2001
21-12-2007
12-12-2008
unknown
01-12-1997
26-10-1997
26-03-2000

THE SCHENGEN BORDER-FREE AREA

Twenty-two EU countries, plus non-EU members Iceland, Norway, Switzerland and Liechtenstein, are part of the Schengen agreement. This allows most people to travel freely from country to country without having to show their passport or get a visa to enter other Schengen nations.

EU: DID YOU KNOW?

The EU is the largest economy in the world. Because of its success in reducing tensions and conflicts between nations, the EU received the Nobel Peace Prize in 2012. The member states of the EU have their own representatives at the United Nations, but the EU also represents the whole group at the UN.

NOBEL PEACE PRIZE MEDAL

FRIEDRICH SCHILLER

The EU flag has twelve stars. The number is supposed to symbolize perfection and unity, not the number of countries that were EU members in 1986.

The EU has an anthem. It is the "Ode to Joy" from Ludwig van Beethoven's Ninth Symphony, composed in 1823. It uses a poem from 1785 by Friedrich Schiller that describes all humanity as brothers and sisters.

Europe Day is May 9 each year. This honors the first steps toward the EU that began with a speech by Robert Schuman, the French Foreign Minister, on this date in 1950.

The EU's motto is "United in Diversity".

The European Parliament meets in Brussels, Belgium. It has over six thousand employees.

EUROPE DAY CELEBRATION

BRUSSELS FLORAL CARPET

All member states elect members of parliament to represent them at Brussels, and about one third are women. In several EU countries, voting is mandatory.

The first direct election of members of the European Parliament was in 1979. Before that, members of the parliament were appointed by the governments of the member states.

Norway held referendums in 1972 and 1994 to see if its population wanted to join the EU. Both times the "no" side got the larger number of votes.

Robert Schuman, who made the speech that stimulated the beginning of modern European cooperation, was the first president of the European Parliament. He held that position from 1958 to 1960.

ROBERT SCHUMAN

CASTLE OF NEUSCHWANSTEIN, GERMANY

Each EU country has seats in the European Parliament according to the size of its population. Germany, the most populous country in the EU, has 99 MPs out of a total of 751.

European Parliament MPs are elected for five-year terms.

The first two times Great Britain tried to join the EU, in 1963 and 1967, France vetoed the application.

THE WORLD'S GREAT POWERS

The European Union is a powerful force in the world right now, but other great powers have come before it. Read Baby Professor books like Everything You Need to Know About the Rise and Fall of the Roman Empire and The Byzantine Empire to learn more about Europe and the world's history.

Visit
BABY PROFESSOR
EDUCATION KIDS
www.BabyProfessorBooks.com
to download Free Baby Professor eBooks
and view our catalog of new and exciting
Children's Books